WHEN OPPORTUNITY KNOCKS...

MAKE SUCCESS HAPPEN

WHEN OPPORTUNITY KNOCKS...

MAKE SUCCESS HAPPEN

Kim Elliott

NEW HARBOR PRESS

RAPID CITY, SD

Elliott/New HarborPress
1601 Mt. Rushmore Rd, Ste 3288
Rapid City, SD 57701
www.newharborpress.com

Ordering Information:
Quantity sales. Special discounts are available on quantity purchases by corporations, associations, and others. For details, contact the "Special Sales Department" at the address above.

When Opportunity Knocks/Elliott. -- 1st ed.
ISBN 978-1-63357-198-3

Where scriptures are used...

"Scriptures quoted from the Holy Bible, New Century Version©, copyright ©1987, 1988, 1991 by Thomas Nelson, Inc. Used by permission."

Other Books by Kim Elliott:
When Opportunity Knocks...Hold Hands ©2015 by Outskirts Press

This little book of ramblings is dedicated to my work family in Parks and Recreation and to anyone else who wants to be successful.

May they enjoy and maybe understand a little more as to why I behaved the way that I did!

—Just the Boss

Contents

Preface 1

1. When Staff Complain 7

2. When to Discipline 13

3. When Staff Does Good 19

4. When Staff Mess Up 25

5. When Staff Need Praise 31

6. When Your Boss Messes Up................................ 37

7. When Your Boss Needs Praise............................ 43

8. Lifting Spirits... 49

9. Listen to Your People....................................... 55

10. Smile While You Work 61

11. Listen to What is Going On Around You 67

12. Managing your Most Important Resource 73

13. Time To Keep Your Mouth Shut........................ 79

14. To Move Forward...Take Two Steps Back........... 85

15. When Cutting Hot Peppers, Don't Rub Your Eyes Before Washing Your Hands 91

16. Pearly White Teeth 97

17. Change Happens...Manage, Don't Manipulate 103

18. Don't Follow the Pendulum............................. 109

19. Remember Who Your Boss Really Is 117

20. Keep the Culture..123

21. Don't Surround Yourself With "Yes" People 127

22. Following Regulations...133

23. Make Your Staff (and Your Boss) Look Good 139

Epilogue 143

*One Day
You Will Look Back
and Realize
That It Was
The Little Things In Life
That Actually Were the Big Things In
Life!*

Preface

WHEN I STARTED TO write my previous book, *When Opportunity Knocks...Hold Hands*, I had no idea that I would do more than just pen a few paragraphs that might be beneficial to our kids. My first book was a result! As I wrote, more and more thoughts kept coming into my mind that I felt might also be beneficial.

This is being written not just to bosses, but to anyone that might become a boss and wants to be successful. Included in this group are ministry teams and pastors. At the same time, this is not designed to be a deep theological dissertation on the meaning of being successful in business or organizations. The intent is for the individual to receive the encouragement to do the right thing in their own business operations. At the same time, some scripture references with thoughts have been provided to help your understanding and study. The book of Proverbs in the Old Testament is full of verses that would be beneficial for business, management, and being a boss. However, I believe the ones listed will help you to possibly see another side to being successful and productive.

Keep in mind that I have not covered every possible situation with having a productive and successful business. Realistically...no one could. I have only included little snippets, or ideas of what might help you to start your journey. I do believe that I have provided some of the most common situations, though. Others might be provided in another book, at another time!

People have led and managed people for thousands of years. Some would say that aspects of leadership have changed over those years and that we need to adapt our leadership styles to keep up with the times. I am not so sure that leadership and management styles have changed. It may be just the names of certain leadership and management aspects that have changed. However, technology and culture changes do occur and yes, we probably need to make some adaptations to some of those changes, but...do people actually change?

We know that God does not change (Malachi 3:6)...and...we were made in His image (Genesis 1:27). He (Jesus) is the same yesterday, today and tomorrow (Hebrews 13.8). He does not change with the culture, but He is relevant across cultures. If we are found to be in God's image, then we also should not try to change our image just because the culture around us is changing. God intends something better for us. He is the one who lays out our path according to His Word. His Word has been shown to be true and consistent from the very beginning. His Word is a path for our feet! That path gives us direction. He will not fail us when we follow His path.

If we try and change His Word to fit our culture, we will not be successful. But, someone might say that God intends for us to change as our culture changes around us. My response is that His concept of successful management has been around for thousands of years, and is still valid. If God changes, then He will not be true to His own Word.

As this is being written, we have nine grandchildren! We have raised three children of our own. Our three kids were born in three different states but we can say that all of them were mostly raised in New Mexico, the Land of Enchantment! We have worked in Illinois, Missouri, Texas, Arizona, Maryland and New Mexico. Our jobs have caused us to work with people from all over the United States and at various levels of employment and leadership.

I only say this to point to the fact that we have seen and worked with many different people, from several different cultures, and many different situations. People are still people! Our kids growing up in our house are very similar to our grandkids growing up. Most of the situations they put themselves into are very similar to others as they grow up and mature. The details may be different but the concepts of dealing with people are not.

From a business standpoint, the concepts of growth with success are very similar. What you do and how you act within your business workplace is directly related to your success. You build positive relationships at home with your family...and...you build positive working relationships with the people you work with in your business. This includes your boss and the people you are responsible to lead!

Currently, I am retired from full time Parks and Recreation work! But, for the last 40 years of my career in Parks and Recreation, I worked as a Director, Superintendent, Supervisor, Coordinator and Assistant Director of Intramural Sports. I always had people that worked for me and followed my instructions. I can honestly say that I worked with some of the best people in the nation in Parks and Recreation. My staff looked to me for guidance and direction. Did they always find what they were looking for in my example? I would like to say "Yes", but realistically, I know that I failed from time to time. My example might not have always been the best...but, I can say that I tried!

Doing what God has asked of me and being what He wants me to be has been a growth and learning process. This has been a process...being a supervisor of people. I had to learn...listen to my people...and grow with my staff. Most importantly, I also had to grow with God in order to try and bring the best out of my staff.

Of course, I had training to be a good supervisor, leader and manager. But, when I realized that God had already shared His expertise with me on these topics, all that was needed was to look in His Word for the direction and of course the answers.

I would like to think that I have been fairly successful in working with people in my business setting. Some of these people have been more successful than others and what that means is that if my staff have been successful, then I have at least been successful to a certain extent, in leading them.

That is what I want to share with you. I want you to be successful and if some of my experiences can help you to be successful, then I will have accomplished what I set out to do in the beginning!

In my first book, *When Opportunity Knocks...Hold Hands* I placed one business chapter on complaints toward the end of the book as an example of what to look for in this book. I have tweaked it some... and...as I think about the first book, I realized that some of those chapters may also apply in a business setting.

You might say that I have focused on the fact that dealing with people has been the same for thousands of years. That, I do believe is a true statement.

In my first book, *When Opportunity Knocks...Hold Hands*, we chatted about the small things that help to make a positive relationship with the spouse, the kids, and friends. *When the big choices come along, if we have been consistent with the small choices, then making that big choice is a piece of cake!* Being successful in your business is similar.

By the way, if you take the time to answer the questions and look at the scripture references at the end of each chapter, I believe that you will find that they will be an additional benefit to you.

I do need to say a special thanks to my wife, Dee for providing most of my copyediting and to my sister, Michele for reading the manuscript and making suggestions. My wife even wrote one of the sections which I shortened and added additional thoughts.

You should have no problems reading through this book. It is written in conversational language and should be easy to understand. You can read it in one day fairly easy. I have not given you all of the answers, but enough to get you thinking about this topic, possibly setting a foundation, and hopefully to have the desire placed inside to learn more.

Read, enjoy, and be successful when the opportunity arises!

Many times...
all
that someone wants...
is to know that someone
is listening to them.

1. When Staff Complain

I HAVE FOUND THAT adults complain about as much as kids. When you get right down to it, adults seem to complain about the same things as kids . . . but on different levels!

Without looking at specifics, our grandkids have complained about family, friends, not having enough money, having to travel to the store, what to wear, not enough leisure time, homework, doing chores(work), going to bed, getting out of bed, the food they are eating...well I think you get the idea! Adults complain about the same things, only they do it in a more sophisticated manner!

When it comes right down to the nitty gritty about complaints, it is simple to make the connection that when someone complains, they are actually complaining because they are selfish in many ways. As our grandkids want their way, so do we...the adults!

Do I fall into this same category of being selfish? Of course I do!

When one of our kids complains, we then have that opportunity to turn that complaint into a positive. We might grab them by the hand and take the opportunity to chat with them about the positives in life. We try to instill an attitude of gratefulness, instead of never being satisfied.

We can do the same in the corporate culture. In the past, when I found someone complaining on staff, the best thing I could do was just listen. Many times that is all that someone wants...to know that someone is listening to them. Besides, if you listen, you can usually discover the basics of the problem that is causing the complaint. If you understand the basics, then you can more appropriately discern the proper way to address the complaint. Not everyone will always be happy with the result, but at least you cannot be faulted for not listening to your staff.

Turn the complaint into a positive in your work situation. No one wins if complaints are unanswered...and...usually, the situation will just get worse. Use this opportunity to create an atmosphere of peace and well-being with your staff. The end result is that your staff will know and understand that you will address negative situations, but most importantly, you care for your people.

NOTE: The above chapter, with a few changes, appeared in *When Opportunity Knocks...Hold Hands* to give readers a little taste of what would follow in this book.

Scriptures, Thoughts and Questions:

Genesis 3

In the Garden, Adam complained about Eve and Eve about the Serpent. Their actions were counted as sin and God provided punishment...yet He also gave the sons of Adam a way out for the future.

Jonah 4:1-11

Jonah complained because he felt that he knew more than God... but God showed His compassion to a repentant people which Jonah did not like.

Exodus 16:1-21

The people of Israel complained and wanted to go back. However, this was a part of the Boss's plan to provide for the people. When they grumbled, He still provided.

Complaints are Also Opportunities for Success

It is apparent that God listens when we complain...and...oh do we complain! God patiently listens to us while we rant and rave about something that we believe is not fair. Maybe that is all we really need...just to know that He listens. But, when do we start to listen?

Usually, we won't listen until we are through having our say. However, when we are through talking, we then have to take the time to reload our thoughts. That is the time for the boss or supervisor to ask questions about the situation to see if there are others that need to be heard. It is also the time for us to listen!

Chapter One Questions:

1. List the things you find yourself complaining about the most.

2. Have you searched God's Word for help in addressing the issues of the complaint?

3. How, if needed, will you address these issues with your co-worker, friend, supervisor...?

4. As the boss, how do you handle complaints? Do you handle complaints in a manner that would please God... Yourself... or your Staff?

...put together a
"Ten Commandments" for your business.
...Be sure and share your philosophy
with your staff.

2. When to Discipline

JUST BECAUSE YOU HAVE a worker who messes up, does not mean that discipline is required. As with our kids and grandkids, they may do something that is not correct, but discipline would only be applied if it was a willful act, could hurt someone else, either physically, mentally, or spiritually, or if it did not show respect for an individual.

Most businesses have a list of items that, if not followed, will result in someone being disciplined. If you are the Boss and do not have this list, then it should be compiled right away. In other words, put together a "Ten Commandments" for your business. Some businesses will call this a Code of Conduct.

You need to have some idea what the discipline might be before it happens. This should be listed for every item on your list. What is your philosophy of discipline? When is it needed? Are their exceptions? By already having made up your mind, you will be seen in a more positive perspective than if you fiddle around and take too long to make a decision about discipline.

Remember, that when you have to discipline, do it and move on. Do not dwell on the discipline. You want your staff to be more productive and successful. Dwelling on what has just happened will not help to bring about the desired results. Keep in mind that you have to have an understanding of what those desired results might be.

Consistency is important. Keep in mind the act, the proposed discipline, and extenuating circumstances when making a decision. Keep in mind also that you, as the Boss, can make exceptions. Exceptions should also be consistent.

However, before you discipline, make sure you have investigated the situation first to determine if discipline is actually needed and who should be corrected.

Be sure and share your philosophy with your staff. That way, they cannot say they had no idea what the consequences would be if they did something that might need disciplinary action. Also, by sharing your philosophy with staff, you free them to do their jobs without being concerned about violating the rules.

This will help staff to be more productive and successful.

Scriptures, Thoughts and Questions:

Romans 3:23; 6:23

Sin requires a payment even if we repent. This is similar to a business setting. Discipline is a must. God says from the beginning that the payment for sin is death. In regard to business, doing something wrong might be something simple...or...it could be very complex. Each might have it's own penalty.

Hebrews 12:7-11

Discipline should occur because someone wants us to be the best that we can be...as a father is with his child.

Proverbs 12:1

Thoughts are provided when discipline is administered for someone who is intelligent and discipline for someone who is stupid. We should desire discipline if it is provided to help us to be better. If we twist the purpose of discipline, then the end result will not be positive.

Chapter Two Questions

1. In business, is a wrong that has been done considered a sin?

2. What might be the difference between a sin and a wrong doing in business? Would there be anything in business that a wrong doing would be considered a sin?

3. Have you or someone you know been disciplined unfairly? What would you have done differently to correct the situation?

*Productivity is
enhanced
when you have
a positive attitude.*

3. When Staff Does Good

DURING MY YEARS OF leading staff in a municipality, being involved with private, corporate recreation, coaching off and on for many years, working in the college intramural/recreation field, officiating basketball and baseball...and being able to meet and interact with park and recreation professionals from all around the country...I can honestly say that I have had the opportunity to work with some of the best professionals, ever. Now, with that said, I believe that many others will say the same about the people they work with, whether or not they work in parks and recreation or some other field!

We can normally say that they are the best, because someone in a leadership position helped to make them the best. Someone helped them to enjoy their job. Someone showed appreciation for what they were doing. Someone took the time to make sure that staff were trained. Someone made sure that they felt part of the team. Someone recognized them when they did a good job!

Who was that someone?

That someone is a leader...a supervisor...a boss...and...it is you!

Your people will do good things in their work situations. How should they be treated or recognized? Do you just expect your staff to do good, or do you only discipline when they don't?

First of all, does doing something good just mean that someone is more productive? Well...doing something productive can be seen as doing good...but...it is not all. How about getting along with staff? Is that productive? How about helping a newcomer to understand their job better? Can someone be more productive when they understand the basic operation of their job? How about just being positive about your work? If a worker is positive while they work, does that positive feeling/action help that person to be more productive? How about encouraging someone else to do better? How about coming up with a new idea?

Does not all of the above help someone to be more productive? I believe so!

Productivity may be what we want, but what is the best way to get there? I believe that you recognize your people when they do perform well. Productivity is enhanced when you have a positive attitude. It is enhanced when your people get along with their peers. It is enhanced when everyone seems to understand their jobs a little better. When you encourage your staff, productivity improves...or at least has a chance to happen. When your staff works together to try and come up with new ideas to be more productive...productivity improves!

When opportunity knocks...make success happen! Recognize the good in your staff.

Scriptures, Thoughts and Questions:

Genesis 5:18-24

God recognizes good work. He recognized Enoch who was righteous by not allowing him to die.

Genesis 6-9

God recognized Noah and his family for being righteous. Because of Noah's righteousness and because Noah obeyed God, the Boss recognized him over all the others on earth and kept Noah and his family alive during the Flood.

Job 42:10-17

Satan thought that he could cause Job to curse God, but he couldn't, even with all that Satan took from him. Instead, because Job would not curse God for his troubles and losses, God blessed Job with much more than what He had taken from him.

Matthew 25:14-28

In the parable of the Talents, the owner blessed those who did well by giving them more. The one who did not try, had his talent taken from him.

Chapter Three Questions

1. Choose an area in your work environment that needs improvement. What changes can be made by being positive and encouraging rather than negative and demanding?

2. How will you personally encourage employees/coworkers to pursue positive attitudes and creative productivity?

3. What are some methods of recognizing your staff when they do well?

4. List other people in the Old & New Testament who did good. How were they recognized?

*All good people
mess up somewhere
along the way. The
important thing is
to help them keep moving
Forward.*

4. When Staff Mess Up

I KNOW QUITE A few people who haven't messed up in some way, shape, or form for the last several years. However, to be honest with you, they have passed on from this life, the obituary has been written, and they are either sitting on a shelf under their picture or are in a box six feet under with others who have not messed up in years.

Everybody makes mistakes. Our kids and grandkids did, and still do all the time. And, I suppose if you want to be realistic, we do, too! Why?

Kids are growing and maturing. As they grow they see new things that they have not seen or been able to experience, yet. Their power of reasoning has not fully developed to encompass the situations that they may come across in their daily activities. As a result... they make mistakes.

As the kids grow and mature, the natural thing we want them to do as they come across a different or a difficult situation, is to ask, before they get into trouble, or at the very least, make the effort to think through the situation, first. However, once they have grown, we expect them to have already experienced many issues...through emotions, through pain, through observations, through acquiring knowledge, and through their relationships with friends and family.

We still expect them to ask for help, yet...now that they are older, we also desire for them to begin to make their own positive choices. Will our grandkids still mess up? Of course they will. But, we hope with fewer occurrences and less severity of the consequences!

How does our grandkids growing up and also messing up relate to a successful business?

When helping my staff learn their jobs, I knew that it was impossible for me, as their boss, to teach them everything they needed to know to make their efforts a success. I looked for people who could think for themselves. I looked for people who would be innovative in their thought processes. I looked for people who could be successful and productive with a minimum of oversight. I looked for people who were not afraid to ask for help! I looked for people who might take three (3) steps forward and somewhere along the line, they would need to take one (1) step backwards before moving forward again. I looked for people who might have a similar philosophy of work success compared with mine. If I did my "looking" correctly, then general guidance was (is) all that was needed for the new employee.

All good people mess up somewhere along the way. The important thing is to help them to keep moving forward.

In most cases, I can interchange the words staff with kids (or grandkids). A person who can be seen as a successful parent will more than likely apply the concepts of good parenting to their business relationships.

My staff were my kids. They were my family...and...as the head of the household, or Department Head, I had a responsibility to help them to grow and become successful!

Scriptures, Thoughts and Questions:

Romans 15:1-2

Everyone makes mistakes. However, the stronger person should help the weaker or less knowledgeable person to do what is right.

Judges 16:4-30

Samson messed up with Delilah. Samson still had to pay the penalty for his wrong doing, but in the end, God blessed Samson.

Matthew 26:69-75

Peter denied Christ three times in one night. He felt terrible when he finally realized what he had done. The feeling was real, and Peter had to live with it. However, Jesus did not hold it against Peter. He actually sought him out and asked him to "Feed His sheep." Be the leader!

Chapter Four Questions

1. What valuable lesson have you learned from a mistake that you have made?

2. How have you changed the way you deal with staff/coworkers because of this mistake?

3. How will you use your mistake as an opportunity to create a better work environment?

4. List those people in the Old Testament and New Testament who messed up and were able to learn from their mistake.

Simply stated... too much of a good thing is counterproductive.

5. When Staff Need Praise

WHEN YOUR STAFF DOES a good job, they need to be recognized. However, sometimes staff just need to be praised for their work. On the surface, being recognized for doing good and being praised appears to be very similar, but, they are very different.

Praise is more than recognizing a worker for doing well. Praise is higher than recognition. Let's say that recognition is given when someone does something specific that is good. Praise is more general and encompasses more than just a specific act. When recognition can be done with a specific act, praise can be given when someone connects the dots and does the right thing over and over. Praise may be given for something that is more abstract.

A boss sometimes has a staff member who is consistently productive. Sometimes someone makes an effort to get along with other staff. This person is positive in his/her very nature. Sometimes a boss has someone who is very creative or innovative in thought.

These are just a few reasons to praise someone over and above recognition. However, praise can be ineffective!

But, wait! Doesn't everyone like and need praise? How can it be ineffective?

Simply stated...too much of a good thing is counterproductive. At the same time, praise given for a genuine reason, can be very productive. But...that is the key! It must be given for a genuine reason. The employee must feel like there is value attached to the praise. Now when I say "value" I do not necessarily mean monetary value, even though that could be a factor in helping your staff become more productive.

What is meant when I say "value" is that the praise must be genuine and the boss feels like the praise is definitely deserved. Oh! And don't forget that your staff person must also feel the same! Otherwise, it is all for show.

If you want your staff to be successful, make sure your praise is genuine!

Scriptures, Thoughts and Questions:

Luke 21:1-4

Jesus praised the woman who gave all she had as being genuine and blessed her.

Proverbs 31:28-31; 2 Kings 4:1-7

A good woman needs praise. This can be seen by the woman who called out to the prophet Elisha for help when she was unable to pay her dead husband's debts. She took the prophet Elisha into her home. God blessed her by making sure that she had enough oil that she could sell to live and pay her dead husband's debt.

Philippians 1:3-6

Paul gives praise to the Church at Philippi. He prays with joy and thanksgiving.

Chapter Five Questions

1. How do you feel/react when you receive genuine praise?

2. How will you develop an environment where praise is given and received in an effective manner?

3. What are some examples of genuine praise in your work setting?

4. List Old Testament and New Testament people who needed and were given praise.

*If credibility is lost,
then the employee
wonders if they are
in the right job...
with the right boss.*

6. When Your Boss Messes Up

THIS SECTION MAY BE a little difficult to write as a boss, or former boss. People (bosses and parents) don't like to admit that they have messed up. However, the comments about staff messing up in an earlier chapter holds true for the boss, also.

Let us go back to successfully parenting the kids and grandkids.

Parents don't like to admit making mistakes when raising children. But the reality of the situation is actually pretty simple. We do make mistakes! Kids learn from their parents and somewhere down the line, you will see your kids doing exactly what you have done. Kids copy their parents! Workers many times will copy bosses, too!

There has been a time or two (or more) when the kids did something wrong and I really blasted them for it. They should have known better. What were they thinking? Someone could have been hurt. And...other typical comments from a parent or grandparent who are "always" right! The kids protested greatly saying that they were innocent of the act. Of course they tried to explain to me actually what happened, which would prove their innocence, but at first I would seldom listen to the evidence. Why? Because I knew what they had done!

Discipline was about to happen.

Now I have to pause here a second to explain that if the discipline occurs before you find out what actually happened, you might have more of a problem. This is especially true in a business setting. So...what do you do? Naturally, you try and find out what happened, first.

Well, to make a long story short, I really felt bad about blaming one of the kids for doing something that they actually did not do! I messed up! I had to make it right with my kids.

A boss has to make it right with their staff.

If he or she doesn't, then credibility and integrity is lost. If credibility is lost, then the employee wonders if they are in the right job... with the right boss. Staff wonder if what they are doing is right. They do not want to be raked over the coals again for something they did not do! If credibility is lost, then the boss runs the risk of their team not being productive or successful.

You know the bad part of this? The longer the boss does not make it right, the longer they believe that they did the right thing. Credibility issues only get worse! To be more specific, it makes your work situation that much more difficult which in turn may create a negative work environment.

Let's consider another factor. A Boss, when doing the right thing creates an environment that instills faith in the staff. The more "right" things seen by staff to happen because the Boss acts and cares, the more your staff realizes that the Boss can be seen as someone with honesty and integrity. Your staff is more likely to work with you to come up with the correct decision.

What do you do if the boss does not make it right? A good boss will investigate what was done. However, if the investigation does not turn up the truth, then...doing the right thing may be up to you, as the employee, to make sure the Boss considers the truth.

With that said, if you have a boss who will not listen, then your job is more difficult, or, may not even be possible! Let us just consider a boss who desires to do the right thing.

To make a longer story shorter, you, as the boss, must swallow your pride and say you are sorry...or that you were wrong. If discipline is still needed, you need to follow through with it. However, if you have wronged someone, then you need to do the right thing and correct the wrong...whatever that might be...before discipline is carried out.

Then how does the employee respond? If your boss is trying to do what is right, then you should recognize that effort and be as productive as possible in your work day. The boss should apologize for the wrong thinking and you should except the apology and let your boss know that you do appreciate him/her going the extra mile to make things right!

Keep in mind that if you, as the boss, do the right thing, your staff will hopefully also work to do the right thing at some time in the future. Your staff may just make an effort to be more productive because they see their boss trying to do what is right. If you don't do the right thing, then you have just created more problems for yourself in the future.

Be successful by correcting the wrong...at least as best as you can!

Scriptures, Thoughts and Questions:

2 Samuel 11-12

David messed up with Bathsheba when he acted upon his own selfish desire. Even though he repented, David still had to carry the burden of wrong doing...his son died as a result of their sin. However, God blessed David and Bathsheba with another son who became the next King of Israel. The wrongdoer is still responsible for the wrong-doing.

Galatians 2:11-21

Peter had seen in a vision and heard God speaking to him about the house of Cornelius. He saw the results of God blessing the non-Jew with salvation. But when he was with his friends, other Jews, he was afraid to associate with gentiles. God, through Paul, straightened him out and continued to use Peter in the spreading of His Word.

Acts 16

Paul and Silas, while preaching the Gospel, were arrested and thrown into jail. The gentiles messed up because they thought Paul and Silas were just Jews. They failed to check if they were Roman Citizens. They issued the punishment before finding out. After hearing the praises and prayers of Paul and Silas in the jail, God opened all the doors to the prison. After Paul and Silas saved the jailer's life by not escaping, the jailer took them to his house, where he heard the Gospel and his whole household was saved.

Chapter Six Questions

1. Have you ever been wrong? When?

2. Have you ever accused someone of a wrong only to find out later that you made a mistake? When?

3. How will you approach a staff member, or your boss who is wrong?

4. As the boss, how will you make the wrong right?

If
you can interact
with your Boss
on a...positive note, then
you will be more successful.

7. When Your Boss Needs Praise

WHEN SHOULD YOU GIVE praise to your Boss? I guess the first question should be, *"Does my Boss deserve praise?*

What does a boss do that might deserve some praise?

Let's see!

When your boss interacts positively with your coworkers, does that not deserve some praise? When your boss actively tries to get to know you or your coworkers a little better, does that deserve some praise? When your boss clearly explains work goals and directions in a manner that staff can understand, might that be something to be praised? When your boss receives recognition from the Big Boss for doing the right things, might that be something that can be praised?

Does your boss stay on task? Is the mission of the organization being accomplished? Are goals and objectives being met? Is the boss helping you to achieve the mission, goals and objectives?

All of the above might be a good reason to give some praise to your boss.

I can say that if you can find at least something little every now and then to praise, you will find that your interactions with your Boss will be more positive! If you can interact with your Boss on a more positive note, then you will be more successful. And...in the long term, your Boss will also be more successful...and he/she will more than likely to share some of that success with you!

How might this praise be shown? When you work hard, you honor your boss. Your boss will be more productive and they will help you to be more productive or successful.

Scriptures, Thoughts and Questions:

Keep in mind that we have been talking about bosses in regard to business settings, but remember that your overall Boss is God!

He provided the Ten Commandments and the rules and regulations at the Sermon on the Mount. Genuine praise also includes a "Thank You!"

Acts 16; Philippians 1:12-14

Paul praised God even while he was in prison.

Esther 1-10

Esther did the right thing when she went to King Xerxes to make a request for her people. Mordecai did what was right when he encouraged Esther to do what was right. King Xerxes, even though he had signed a proclamation that all Jews could be killed on a certain date, did what was right when he understood what he had done.

Luke 7:1-16

The Roman soldier, no matter what he had done in the past, loved his daughter so much that he went against all accepted practices, and asked Jesus to heal his daughter, which Jesus did.

Luke 17:11-19

Jesus healed 10 lepers, but only one returned to thank Jesus. Can you see this happening in your workplace?

Philippians 2:9-11

Whether we believe it or not, when Jesus comes again, every knee will bow to our King. The King is our boss and praise is given when we bow to Him.

Chapter Seven Questions

1. How can genuinely praising your boss, when merited, create a more positive work environment?

2. When are some occasions to praise your boss, in your specific work situation?

3. What happens to an individual(s) when merited praise is given?

4. What happens to an individual when merited praise is not given?

*...if
the boss is a
positive spirited person
then staff
will more than likely
follow in the boss's footsteps.*

8. Lifting Spirits

IF YOU WORK ALONE, it is very difficult to have your spirits lifted because you do not have a boss (so to speak) and you do not have coworkers. However, most people do not work alone. In most cases, you work with a team to accomplish a common goal, or at the very least you have someone who oversees and reviews your individual work.

You can usually find at least one person who constantly has a smile on their face. That is the person that you want to work beside the one with the negative attitude. Why is this the case?

To put it simply...negative people spread negativity! Positive people spread positive thoughts and positive actions. People do not want to hear negativity all day long. It impairs productivity!

That is a downer!

You can lift spirits by being a positive influence on someone else.

Listen closely about negativity and positivity. It is true that a positive spirit can help to lift someone's negative spirit. But, it is also true that a negative spirit can bring down a positive spirit. As the boss, it is extremely important that you watch very closely your attempt to lift the spirit of a negative person by having a positive spirited person work with the negative spirited person. You do run the risk however, of lowering the spirits of a positive person, but, in my opinion, it is well worth the risk. The interaction of the two employees just has to be monitored.

Also keep in mind, that if the boss is a positive spirited person, then staff will more than likely follow in the boss's footsteps. Productivity will be the result and you will be more successful with your business.

Scriptures, Thoughts and Questions:

If you look at most scripture, God intends to lift us up...lift our spirits by sharing what the future holds. He shares the plan of His salvation. Naturally, He has to also share the reality of the negative sides of life and the results of sin so that we can be encouraged.

Hebrews 12:12-13

Those who are strong should lift up the weak. Stay on the right path.

Psalms 98

Many psalms are written to lift spirits. The spirit is lifted when God is praised.

Acts 16; Philippians 1:12-14

By singing and praising God, Paul and Silas not only lifted their own spirits, but also those of other prisoners. Paul in his written letters shares that he has been blessed by God because he was in prison.

I Timothy 1:15-17; 2:1-7; 6:11-16

Paul shares with Timothy encouragement that will not only lift his spirits, but also those with whom Timothy shares his words. Even Paul's charge to Timothy is designed not only to instruct, but to uplift the spirit.

Chapter Eight Questions

1. Do you bring a positive or negative attitude to your work environment each day?

2. How would you personally help the negative spirited individual become more positive?

3. What things in your work environment can be changed to encourage positive thinking, speaking, and actions?

4. Why is it important for the boss to have a positive attitude at work?

We
may hear them,
but we
cannot understand them!

9. Listen to Your People

SOMETIMES ALL THAT OUR kids want is for someone to listen to what they have to say. That is no different with one of your staff.

Listening to your people can be one of the most productive items that a boss can do. As a matter of fact, this has to be done if you want to be successful! This is of great importance!

Listening to your kids is also one of the most important items on your parenting list. However, if you are a drill sergeant type of parent, or boss and you already know everything that someone might possibly say, the skill of listening is probably not a high priority...but it should be!

It is sometimes hard to understand what our kids are actually trying to say. Their grasp of the English language is not at the level of ours for proper understanding. Sometimes when they are hurt, they try to speak to us by crying and sobbing. We can understand that they are hurt, but they cannot express where or even how bad, or for that matter, how it happened. These are all things that we need to understand in order to help them. So...we have to not only hear, but to listen to what they are trying to tell us.

It is our responsibility to get them to the point where we can understand what they are saying. We may hear them, but we cannot understand them! We need to move on from hearing them, to actually listening with understanding.

Listening to someone, whether it is a child, spouse, friend, or an employee, takes an effort. The word listen is either a verb or a noun according to the dictionary. If we want to listen properly, it takes an effort...that makes it a verb, an action word!

To listen to a staff person, you cannot be distracted by someone else, a process that is underway, something you are reading, or even a problem of your own. Your staff person deserves your undivided attention so the issue can be heard by you and hopefully be resolved.

Resolving issues is what you want for your operation to be successful. When you take the time to actually listen to your people, they will feel like you care about what is happening at work, or even in their own personal lives. The more you care about your people and take the time to listen to them, the chances are very positive that you will be that much more successful in your business operation.

Scriptures, Thoughts and Questions:

Psalms 40:1-3

If we are patient God will hear our cry and respond. When He does, our very thoughts will be changed with a new song. When we know that God has listened to us, then our attitude will be changed.

I Kings 3:16-28

When you listen to what someone says, you can actually read between the lines. Also, when listening to both sides of the story, you have a better idea of what is truth. Because Solomon listened, the people saw him as a wise leader.

John 10:3-5

Sheep pay attention to someone they trust. Not unlike sheep, employees, or staff will also pay more attention to a boss who is seen to be one who listens to their problems and rejoices in their good times.

Proverbs 12:15

Listen to your people and provide good counseling, and you will be seen as a wise person.

Chapter Nine Questions

1. What are some ways that you can become engaged in listening?

2. What is the difference between an active listener and a passive listener?

3. How does listening to your people affect them?

4. Would a regular time set aside to chat with staff be helpful?

Your smile
may be
just what is needed to
promote productivity
in your business.

10. Smile While You Work

Throughout these chapters, you might find a simple thread that stands out. That thread is a thread of positivity.

Being positive in your work, or in your relationships with staff, customers, bosses and anyone else that might come along has the potential to make you happy. Most happy people smile while working. It is like the seven dwarves who "Whistle While You Work!" They are happy!

Why do the dwarves whistle while they work in the Disney film *Sleeping Beauty*? It shows a positive attitude that spills over to their work. They are more productive when they express their positive attitude by whistling! In other words, they smile while they whistle... while they work!

To smile at work expresses that positive attitude. Chances are you will also be more productive while you work, just like the dwarves.

Another example maybe a little closer than the dwarves, is to smile when you talk on the telephone. Why? The person on the other phone can actually "feel" the smile as they listen.

A comment was made in another chapter that smiling can be infectious to your staff. Smiling may affect other staff...even staff who are negative. Your smile may be just what is needed to promote productivity in your business.

There may be another reason for someone to smile while working.

How do you combat going to work when you really don't want to work? Just the act of smiling may be enough to help change your attitude about working that day. Consider this...that if a smile might help to change your attitude, maybe...just maybe, it will be enough to help change your coworkers attitude. Maybe even your boss!

The most important smile is the smile that you bring to the table. You can determine what your attitude will be when you leave the house. Remember that just a simple smile as you work has the potential to help you and your business be successful!

Scriptures, Thoughts and Questions:

I Thessalonians 5:16-18

You can't say this verse any better than the way you find it in I Thessalonians. This is a good place for a smiley face Emoji!

Proverbs 15:13

Happiness makes you smile but if you let sadness take over your life, your spirit will be broken.

James 5:13; Psalm 98:4-8

What is the natural result of being happy? Singing praises and making music is the result. This affects the entire body.

Ecclesiastes 5:19-20

When you speak to others with joy in your heart, you can't help but smile.

Chapter Ten Questions

1. How do you determine if a smile is genuine and heart generated?

2. Is it ever OK to express negative feelings when working? Why...or why not?

3. How can you speak to others with joy in your heart?

4. If you are happy, what does that do to co-workers?

*...we
do a lot more of not paying attention
than...
we would actually like to
admit.*

11. Listen to What is Going On Around You

WITH THE KIDS, WE as parents and grandparents many times just hear noise. It irritates us. It grinds on our nerves. It affects our very psyche. After a while, we get used to the 'noise'. Why does it do this to us?

Simply put, we are not listening, or paying attention to what is actually being done.

I have a feeling that we do a lot more of not paying attention than what we would actually like to admit. It is amazing how this also applies to a business setting, and not just our kids.

Some employees are very talkative. Some are fairly quiet. Some only speak when someone speaks to them. Are your employees actually communicating with one another? Sometimes, yes...and sometimes, no! How can you tell?

You need to know your staff. You need to understand what type of hardships they are going through. You need to understand the joys of their life! Your staff speak to you on a daily basis...though maybe not with their words! You have to train yourself to listen and pay attention to what is going on...whether or not they are actually using words or whether they are using their actions.

When you get to know your staff, you can hear what they are saying...even when they are silent. A great example of this silence can be found in the Simon and Garfunkel song, *The Sound of Silence*. You can tell a lot by listening to the *Sound of Silence*. It would pay the boss, or you to listen to and understand the words to this song. What does the lyrics to this song say? How does it apply to your business?

The people's silence as they go throughout life tell a story. The Boss should be listening!

Listen to the silence to hear if one of your staff needs help in their job. Listen to the silence to see if one of your staff is having problems with other staff. Listen to the silence to see if one of your staff needs you to provide some assistance.

It is funny how listening to the silence in your workplace might be the key to your workplace being more productive.

Of course, as you listen to the silence in your workplace, you also want to listen to the actions of your staff. Listening to silence is like listening to actions. Both can be very revealing.

Is someone moping around while doing their job? Does someone laugh too much? Is someone always late to work? Does someone always sound negative in their written communication? Does it appear that someone is being harassed? Do people whisper a lot when someone, possibly you, are in the room?

How do you as a boss try to bring productivity to your workgroup, when your staff's actions are getting in the way of success? Again, you have to know what is happening with your team. When you understand what is happening, you have that opportunity to correct the problem.

Knowing your people will help you to be more successful as a boss, but...most of all, knowing your people will help your team to be more productive and successful.

Scriptures, Thoughts and Questions:

Ecclesiastes 9:17

Someone has to make an effort to listen to what a wise man says. Just because someone speaks loudly does not mean that they know what is being said.

Psalms 19:1-4

The world around us, though not with the spoken word, speaks volumes, about the creator. Every sunset, every mountain, every lake, every cloud speaks about the maker. Sometimes the creation even talks about mankind and that it is waiting patiently for the new earth.

Psalms 46:10

In order to hear God, one has to be still and listen.

John 1-20

Jesus spoke a lot to us through His silence. He wants us to pay attention to what happens around us. He wants us to pay attention to His ministry. He also wants us to pay attention to the people who are lost and their silence which is all around us. The book of John is good about sharing people's silence.

Luke 22:24-36

Apostles were soon to be leaders in spreading the Gospel. They did not do a good job of paying attention to what was going on during Jesus's ministry. In a sense they failed until they understood what Jesus was doing in their lives. For example, Jesus did not have to talk to the widow who gave what she had in the Temple. Her example was what they saw.

Chapter Eleven Questions

1. How do you react to the sounds of silence?

2. What information can someone in charge gather when they listen to their staff?

3. Does everything require a quick fix...or...are some situations better managed with time?

4. What does God want us to listen for in our lives?

5. What does the silence of God's creation say to us?

*If
you do not provide
the proper resource
that you need for the
job, then
your job may not get
completed with the
desired result.*

12. Managing your Most Important Resource

WHAT IS YOUR MOST important resource in a business? Is it money? Is it your car? Is it your office setup? Is it the materials that are needed to provide your product? Though all of these are important, the most important resource that you have are your people...the people that you work with and the people that work for you! These are all individual resources.

Our grandkids (and of course our kids) are precious in our eyes! We understand that if for some reason we do not do a good job of parenting, our future is in jeopardy! Our legacy, or from a business perspective, our future success all rides on how we manage our greatest resources...our kids or your staff.

Managing your greatest resource can be very tricky because people have different backgrounds, different likes, different cultures, different knowledge bases, different personalities, different... well...almost everything is different! In fact, you can not find two people who are exactly alike...even twins!

So, managing your greatest resource may also be your greatest challenge!

You have a certain job or task that needs to be done to make your business productive. It is your responsibility to align your resources so that this job can be successful. Yet, your greatest resource is made up of many different skills, knowledge and abilities, wants and desires.

Most of these people resources desire to be successful. It is your job to help them. However, those that do not want to be successful... well...it is your job to try and help them, too!

How do you match the job with the best resource? If you take the above logic of helping them, then...that means you have to train your staff to provide them with the details of the job and of the task before them. This is extremely important.

However, there is another way to match the job with the best resource.

As the boss, don't you already know the job to be assigned? You can reduce your training budget by hiring the best fit for the job. When you interview, be sure and ask the proper questions so that you can hire the correct person, or resource for the task ahead. You will only ask for trouble if you do not employ staff with the specific tasks needed for the job to be properly performed and completed. Too many people hire friends, or people who are great resources in areas other than what you need. This can and potentially will be problematic in your system. If you do not provide the proper resource that you need for the job, then your job may not get completed with the desired result. You will not be successful, let alone productive.

You also might find yourself with a resource that is now negatively aligned with you and your business.

With that said, you have to consider many other issues when managing your greatest resource. Your staff has to get along...the teams you have must be able to be inclusive, as well as creative and innovative.

In other words, your greatest resource will also make or break your business. If you manage this resource in a positive manner, then your business will very likely be productive and successful.

Take care of these resources!

Scriptures, Thoughts and Questions:

Romans 12:1-8; I Corinthians 12; Ephesians 4:11

Followers of Christ are different, yet we all make up the Body of Christ. Some of us have different spiritual gifts, yet we are all one body. As the body has different functions for it's parts, so is the Body of Christ. Successful businesses are also made up of many different people all working together for one purpose, with one vision.

Matthew 10:2; Luke 6:12-13

Jesus chose 12 apostles who would be able to help Him in His ministry. Each of these 12 individuals had different gifts, came from various backgrounds, with varied gifts and abilities. Yet Jesus chose 12 to be His disciples and carry the load of what needed to be accomplished...naturally with His help.

Chapter Twelve Questions

1. Review your employees attributes, characteristics, and the jobs they do. Are some of your staff better suited to perform someone else's duties?

2. If so, will you make the change or keep things status quo?

3. Will training for specific job responsibilities be sufficient?

4. What does it take to look past your friends for a job and focus on the requirements for the job instead?

5. Can you teach someone to do a job that you need to be completed? Is the time and effort productive? What factors are involved in this decision?

*...if
there is a time to keep
your mouth shut,
then
there is also a time to
speak.*

13. Time To Keep Your Mouth Shut

PARENTS AND GRANDPARENTS ARE constantly having to tell their kids to "Be quiet!" I think that we just want some peace and quiet sometimes! But, what we are actually telling the kids, is that there is a time to keep your mouth shut...and...a time to open your mouth and share your wisdom...or lack of it.

This also applies to your staff...and probably even to the boss!

Now, I am in favor of being truthful. You only set yourself up for problems if you are not truthful in family and work relationships. However, does being truthful mean that you have to share everything?

It is possible that a boss does not have to share everything. I believe that is a true statement. Is the comment work related? Will it uplift and encourage your staff? Will it help your staff to be more productive?

Keep in mind that if there is a time to keep your mouth shut, then there is also a time to speak.

In my previous job as a municipal employee, the City Manager asked me a couple of times on separate instances if I felt that my counterpart in a different department was doing the job assigned. I did not want to express that I felt like the individual had overstepped their responsibility, so I answered in a very tactful manner, which I felt was also true, but not the whole truth. I answered that, "Everyone sees things from different perspectives."

I thought the situation was solved.

If we take a closer look at this example, we can see that the Boss did not necessarily have a responsibility to tell me the complete truth as to why he was asking if the other individual might have overstepped their bounds. And...I am not sure that I would have actually changed my response to him. I usually tried to stay positive in my responses. In this instance he did not say anything negative about the individual, because that would not have been a positive or productive approach in this situation. However, if I would have shared more of my truthful feelings about the situation, then my boss might have handled the situation on a different level or in a different manner. The decisions that were made did affect me several years later in a negative manner when I originally thought that I was just trying to help. It was my time to speak and I kept quiet!

Scriptures, Thoughts and Questions:

Even Jesus did not share everything clearly with his disciples. He spoke in parables. He only spoke what was necessary about the coming Kingdom...just enough so His followers could do their job...just enough not to take away faith and trust in the Boss...just enough for the individual to listen, think, grow, and learn...and be productive!

Ecclesiastes 3:7

There is a time to speak and a time to keep silent...everything has its time. Keep the balance and remember that there is a time for everything!

I Corinthians 13:1-13

There will come a time when we are perfect and that perfection will also bring understanding.

Chapter Thirteen Questions

1. Does your speech negatively impact your work environment?

2. What kind of speech filtering do you use before mentioning something that may produce questionable results?

3. Does being truthful mean that you need to share everything?

*It is
the larger picture
that gives
the overall project
focus.*

14. To Move Forward...Take Two Steps Back

HAVE YOU EVER BEEN stuck on a project or maybe you have had writer's block! This book is an example of that!

I sit down to write and my mind races with ideas! I would like to say that all of my ideas are great...but...that is not the case. Anyway, I sit down to write with all of these ideas and then I have to sort out the good from the bad. Then I have to look at those good ideas and for some reason, they do not all follow the direction that has been set for this book....so...I discard those good ideas for another time...and hope...that I still have an idea or two left!

Sometimes it seemed like I was not going forward with this writing!

What does an artist do when he or she seems to reach an impasse? They take a step or two back so they can view the larger project. From a successful business aspect, so should the businessman. Why?

It is the larger picture that gives the overall project focus. If you don't step back, you are like the blind men who all describe the elephant by only feeling a part of the animal. One says it is like a snake when feeling the trunk...another says it is a wall...a third feels the legs and says it is like a tree trunk...and the last feels the tail and says it is like a broom. Without seeing the entire picture, you do not know how all the parts fit together.

What happens when you step back to look at the larger picture? You see an elephant!

First of all, the many great ideas that you have can be quickly narrowed down. Some just won't fit with the current project. Some just seem to be better off if you take them in a different direction. Those that are left may be just right, or they may need to be narrowed down even more for the project. Some ideas may connect to a different part of the project, but in a different manner or perspective.

Secondly, you may find that what you are trying to do is too big. Focus will be lost. It may be best to break the project into several pieces in order to be productive. Sometimes it is best just to do one thing at a time...and make sure that it is done correctly before moving on to the next. Seeing the big picture helps us to see what the next step is or the path ahead more clearly.

Thirdly, by stepping back a ways and taking a look at what is being completed, you can see how the various parts will fit in the overall finished project. An artist may check to see if the colors chosen are still best for the overall finished project or if that arm being painted is better located in a different place.

For all practical purposes, taking a step back helps us to evaluate the project from another perspective. We can see if we have gone too far. We can see if parts are missing. We can even see if we should be moving in a different direction. And, we can also see if we need to scrap what we have started and start over again.

Pushing forward on a project may not always be best to be successful! You won't know that if you don't take a step back to see the bigger picture.

Keep in mind that you must stay focused. But on what do you stay focused? Simply put...it is the vision of the business.

Scriptures, Thoughts and Questions:

Matthew 6:33; Matthew 18:11

Jesus gave us our focus. It is to seek God's kingdom and to do what He wants. We do this while also seeking to bring the lost to Jesus.

Genesis 1:27-31; Genesis 6:5-22

God created the Heavens and Earth and Man. He proclaimed what He had created to be "good"! God reassessed what He had made and realized that man, in his sinful nature, had turned wicked. He decided to destroy what He had made and start over with Noah and his family.

Chapter Fourteen Questions

1. How can taking a step back either change or confirm your perspective on the project you are working?

2. Is it necessary for all parties involved in a project to have the same perspective?

3. Why or why not?

4. What happens when you evaluate your project and you know that you should probably start over, but you think that you can fix it instead?

How many steps
does it take
(to lead to Success)?

15. When Cutting Hot Peppers, Don't Rub Your Eyes Before Washing Your Hands

IF YOU LIVE IN the Southwest, it is only a matter of time before you do something stupid like handle or cut up a hot pepper...and then rub your eyes. Your shortcut from cutting to rubbing brings a terrible sensation of burning! Why? It is because you left out a step between the cutting and cooking. You left out the washing of the hands which has to come before rubbing the eyes!

Many things require a process. Step 2 follows Step 1...Step 12 comes before Step 13...and the final step can not occur until Steps 1 thru 47, or something else happen in order. What is your process? How many steps does it take? Who determines the process or the number of steps needed to be successful?

There are several ways to answer these questions.

First of all, you, the boss can determine the steps needed for the process. Sometimes, the boss might ask the staff to do this. However, if you have never put a process or a plan together, it will probably be best to ask for help. Hopefully, your boss or place of business has provided some useful training in this area to help the staff be productive. To be successful, ask. There is nothing wrong with asking for help, especially if you have not had that type of experience or training. It might be wise, to run your thoughts by your supervisor/ boss to make sure the direction you are going, is the same direction they want to go.

You may find that your boss tells you the process that is desired. Again, if you need help, do not hesitate to ask for help, or clarification of the request. The boss may desire a set process because they may want certain types of data when finished. It might be wise to run this process by your boss just to make sure you have it right.

Sometimes the employer may have a set process to follow. This may provide some consistency with the process. What has happened here is that at some time the bosses took a step back to see the bigger picture and decided that they wanted the overall process to be the same for their needs to be productive. However, this does not normally remove individual work within the process. Individuals can still be creative and innovative as they work for the larger goal.

Barring any specific data that your boss may need, your team may sit down to determine the parts of the process that they believe will help everyone to be a success. Keeping in mind that some parts of the process still have to be completed in an order, the overall process can still have a lot of creativity.

Just remember to wash your hands after cutting the hot peppers and before you need to rub your eyes! You will find that success may not burn in this instance!

Scriptures, Thoughts and Questions:

Hebrews 10:12

This was God's plan all along...to make sure that Jesus was proclaimed Lord of All. However, Jesus had to follow the Plan and sacrifice Himself before he could sit at God's right hand.

Matt 10: Luke 10

Jesus gave instructions to His apostles and sent them out and He also gave instructions to the Seventy and sent them out. He gave specific instructions as to what they should do.

Acts 16:6-10

Paul wanted to spread the Word to Asia, but the plan was for Paul to head toward Macedonia. What might have happened if Paul had not listened to God?

2 Peter 3

God plans ahead. He does things in His time, not ours. We see that His Word is fulfilled. We don't normally like to wait when someone makes a promise to us, but God keeps all of His promises and in the order He desires. Look at all the prophecies of Jesus from Genesis to Revelation.

Yes, it is evident that God has a plan...and He is in the process of completing that plan in His order...in His time...with us. And if we try and change the order of His Plan, we will encounter unrest and chaos!

We don't like to wait for end results. But...when we do proper planning for our business, the end result may take time because the process takes time. If we have done our planning, keeping in mind that this process needs to be completed in the proper order, the end result will most likely be positive.

Chapter Fifteen Questions

1. How important is it to share and collect ideas from all who are involved in a project?

2. Is it important for everyone to be on the same page at the same time?

3. Someone still has to make a final decision to go forward or move back. Who might that be in your business?

You
will not be seen as a
successful manager
if
you cannot have your
staff focus on the
vision of your work
and the direction they
need to head.

16. Pearly White Teeth

As PARENTS, CHILDREN CAN sure be frustrating at times, can't they? At the same time, kids think their parents do not know what they are talking about!

A child brushing his or her teeth can only see themselves in the mirror. They see pearly white teeth. There is nothing wrong with the teeth they see. Why brush?

The parent sees their child age in the mirror in front of them. They see pearly white teeth, also...that is, if the vision is one of proper dental care. They see ugly, rotting teeth, if the child refuses to brush regularly. The child's vision of the future is very narrow. The parent sees the possibilities of the future because of experience.

Who has a better vision?

Planning for the future is extremely important, especially in business.

Your staff, at least in typical situations with some exceptions, will probably be made up of both men and women and probably with a range of young and older! You may also have staff who are new to the business and those who have been around for a while. This diversity in workers also may bring a diversity in vision for the future.

This diversity in vision falls on you as the boss. Your business should have a vision as to what the work of the business should be and the direction your business is heading. To be successful, everyone on board must have this vision. You will not be seen as a successful manager if you cannot have your staff focus on the vision of your work and the direction they need to head.

The only way for you to be successful in your management is to help your staff see and agree to take your vision to heart. If this cannot be done, help your staff to find another place where their vision can be supported.

Let us plan to keep our vision of pearly, white teeth one of our assets.

Scriptures, Thoughts and Questions:

Galatians 1:3-10: 3:1-20

God had a plan. God had the vision to see what happens in the future and His Word is given so that we might also see a bit of what is to come. His people were given the law to help them "brush their teeth"! The law was given to point people to Jesus which was provided to help God's people everywhere have a clearer vision.

Isaiah 53; Other Old Testament Prophecies

God had a plan from the very beginning when Adam and Eve were in the Garden. His plan also extends past the Resurrection to the Second Coming of Christ. The prophecies in Isaiah 53 pick up when Jesus is on the earth.

Hebrews 1

More details of God's vision.

I Pet. 1-20

More details of the Plan which identifies us as a person with a new birth and a new Hope which is living through the Resurrection of Christ. God's plan from the beginning continues through His Church on earth all the way through the Second Coming.

Luke 19:10

Vision of Christ is to seek and to save the lost. This is God's Plan from the very beginning.

Chapter Sixteen Questions

1. How do you express your Vision for your business to your staff/employees?

2. If your business is headed in the wrong direction, how do you get your Vision back on track?

3. How do you, as a boss, keep your staff focused on the future?

*It is possible
that there is more
than one way to do a
job.
New employees need
guidance...
Not Manipulation!*

17. Change Happens... Manage, Don't Manipulate

CHANGE IS INEVITABLE!

Again, let's use the example of the kids. As they are growing and maturing, change occurs...and I am not talking about the change needed before being potty trained. Even though that might be another topic for successful management..."Potty Training Staff"!

Growth and maturity is the change that happens! Not only in kids, but in adults, too! When those adults are your staff, it is your responsibility to guide that growth. However, sometimes we want to manipulate the growth, instead.

New employees need guidance. When you employed someone new, you went through the process of interviewing that person. You asked important questions which they answered. You recommended for hire, or hired the person that you felt would be the best fit for the business. That person probably did not have all the knowledge or the skills needed for the job, but you felt and saw the potential to benefit the business.

The word manipulate has several meanings...some can be considered as good but when we consider the word itself, it is usually found in a negative context. However, we can maneuver or manipulate our vehicle through a mine field. That is good! We can influence someone's life for good. That is good!

We can control or manipulate someone's actions to suit us. That is not good! We can direct or affect (manipulate) someone's choices that will benefit us and not them. That is not good!

When someone new is employed, you want them to be successful. You hired them to do the job because of their skills, knowledge and abilities...their potential. It is possible that there is more than one way to do a job. The new person may find a new way to get the work done more efficiently that is even better than your way. It might just be possible that you can manipulate a new employee to the point that will influence them enough that they never find a new, more efficient way...a way which will make you look good as the boss!

So, when change happens, encourage your team to meet the challenge of the change with their skills, their abilities, and their knowledge. The end result may be more productivity and increased success for your business.

Scriptures, Thoughts and Questions:

Matthew 28:1-7

The angel said that Jesus was no longer in the tomb. He had risen. This was a huge change. This change resulted in Jews and Gentiles becoming followers of Jesus. This change resulted in the beginning of the Church. This change allowed for the coming of the Holy Spirit. A brand new culture was created with the resurrection of Jesus.

2 Samuel 11:1-5

When David had sex with Bathsheba, a change occurred. David changed his style of leadership from managing to manipulation. He did not want people, and especially Uriah, Bathsheba's husband, to know that he had committed adultery. He tried to manipulate the situation, but found that things just got worse. His manipulation turned from one bad situation into another and the end result was that David eventually had to admit his guilt and take the resulting punishment.

Acts 15:1-2

There were Jewish believers who were saying that the non-Jewish believers had to be circumcised to be a follower of Jesus. Paul tried to reason with the Jewish believers by explaining to them what God was doing with the Gentiles by bringing them into the Church. When reasoning was not successful, they went to Jerusalem to discuss the situation with the leadership. They sought out the answers from others in a discussion and then shared the answer with all believers by communicating their decision to them by letter. The

Jewish believers had tried to manipulate the non-Jewish believers, but calmer voices prevailed. The situation ended up positive because the situation was managed and not manipulated.

Chapter Seventeen Questions

1. What changes occurred as the result of the Resurrection of Jesus?

2. How do you view change in your workplace?

3. Is change always for the better? Explain?

4. Examine your leadership style. Are you a manager, a leader, or a manipulator?

5. Can you list someone who has (or had) a tendency to manipulate both in scriptures and at your work?

*Old
does not mean
Obsolete and New
does not mean
it is Better.*

18. Don't Follow the Pendulum

NOTE: Mostly written by Dee Elliott and edited by the author.

You can find just about anything in the Smithsonian Institute, which is a collection of national museums and research centers in Washington, D.C. administered by the government. The Institute was founded in 1846 for the *increase and diffusion of knowledge* for the nation. When I have visited the nation's capital, I almost always take the time to visit at least one of the Smithsonian museums. I have always enjoyed learning something new!

Learning something new is important. Training new and existing staff is needed for a business to be more productive and successful.

Let's go back to the Smithsonian for a moment.

There used to be a large pendulum in the Smithsonian's Museum of American History. I believe that it has been removed as of this writing for various reasons...but it made an impact on my life. I could stand and watch that pendulum swing back and forth for the longest time.

Pendulum's swing back and forth! That is what they do. Pendulum swings provide an example of what has happened with methods, knowledge and ideas throughout history. Let me give an example of what we might be looking at when I say "don't follow the pendulum! You will not make any progress. You will only move back and forth!"

In my opinion, the most glaring example of following the pendulum that hurts productivity and success can be found in education. Pendulum swings occur in the make-up of content areas, methodology, instructional delivery, discipline, values and ethics, assessment and evaluation...all carried out under titles such as: "innovative", "modern", "current research", "standards and benchmark based", "common core", "teacher assessed", "test performance standards"...the list goes on and on.

If, in reality, the quality of instruction and student learning did improve with every fifteen to twenty year educational pendulum swing, American students would be excelling in every area of academia! As such, American students and teachers are held hostage by a flawed system of education that sways and bends with every political change and is driven by the power of money.

Millions of dollars are spent training educators in the fine art of test taking thus producing student evaluations that will support excellent teacher evaluations which will in turn create superior principal and school evaluations which are then utilized to rank the school district administration as "highly effective" in order to acquire what...more money!

Therefore, the usefulness of educational content is stymied by the current trend and students become the guinea pigs of "someone's" less useful and nonsensical "innovative" curriculum that may, or may not be as effective as the previous.

The pendulum swings, but it does not always bring success.

In considering training staff, let's use an example of ten people. Let us say that these ten are fairly typical of the population. Two or three might be a little below average and need encouragement. Four to six might be average. The other two or three are probably high achievers. These ten people are individuals and need to be encouraged in possibly ten different ways to achieve maximum education, training benefits, and positive job productivity.

The pendulum swings from one "successful" way of instruction/ training to another "successful" way of instruction/training. Each with its own strengths and weaknesses. The pendulum swings from extreme to extreme...one to the other. When it does, one extreme is praised and the old, which seemed to work well, is now obsolete, and therefore discarded. Both extremes of the pendulum swing may be good for a majority of your people, but is that what you want? You want to educate and train all of your staff. Remember, it is not all or nothing!

If both ends of the pendulum swing show a successful way of instruction/teaching, how can all of a sudden, one of the methods become no longer relevant to the educational process?

If one pendulum swing is helpful for a certain type of instruction that helps a certain percentage of students or staff...and the other swing is helpful for another type of instruction that helps another percentage of students, then it would seem that the correct thing to do would be to combine the best from the two worlds and not throw one system out every 15-20 years, or sooner, just because it is seen to be obsolete or old. Plus, there is a lot of money that could, and would be saved.

Oh! And what else might be saved? It might be our students, staff and our entire educational system...or your entire business model!

Old does not mean obsolete and new does not mean it is better. A combination of both seems to be the best for success. Just keep in mind that your success in business can also be affected by pendulum swings.

Scriptures, Thoughts and Questions:

Jeremiah 31:31

God said in Jeremiah and other places that He will execute a new agreement with the people of Israel. God did not say that He was going to throw the old out...He just said that He would make a new agreement. What God did was to fulfil the Old and blended it with the New. He based the New on the foundations of the Old.

Revelation 21:1-4

We will have a better understanding as to what Jesus says about a new heaven and a new earth, if we have taken the opportunity to learn as much as we can about the Heaven and earth that we currently are a part, keeping in mind that He originally created the world to last forever when He called it "Good"!

Isaiah 66:22

When the new heavens and earth arrive, the old will not be forgotten.

Matthew 13:52

A teacher uses both the old and new ideas to get ideas across to their students.

Luke 22:20

The new Christian uses the Old Testament to help understand the New. Jesus explained the new agreement by folding that understanding within knowledge of the Passover Meal to help their understanding of a new agreement. Jesus built upon the Passover.

Chapter Eighteen Questions

1. Is it important to embrace every new idea that comes along in order for you to have a successful business?

2. Where does something new come from?

3. Is something new always better?

4. How do you discern what is best practices for your employees?

5. Is it important to know and understand the past in an effort to move forward?

6. How does embracing the new affect your management style?

*...as you
listen to your boss,
you
might find that
you
will have an
opportunity to help
your boss
be the best!*

19. Remember Who Your Boss Really Is

HAVE YOU EVER FELT like you have two bosses? Which one do you follow? At least, in this world, you are pulled and encouraged to go in two different directions. There are times when our kids, and now our grandkids seem to be two different people.

The question at work is, "Who is my boss?" Which one do I respond to when necessary? Your boss may not know who that person actually is! This is a very difficult situation for an employee or staff person to find themselves.

Sometimes bosses just want to be friends with their staff. This seems like the ideal situation for an employee. However, being friends with the boss, can be very difficult. An employee might expect special considerations from the boss...because of friendship. For that matter, so might the boss! These special considerations, which can also be labeled as favors, can destroy a business and relationships between boss and employee.

The other side of the coin can be just as devastating, if the boss is not considered a friend. Bosses can be seen as unfeeling and uncaring. Who wants to work for a boss that is unfeeling and uncaring?

Balance is what is needed. The real question is, "What kind of boss do I want to be?"

And, of course...you still have to determine who your boss really is.

Your boss deserves respect. Your boss deserves a willingness to help them to be successful. Your boss deserves your effort to do your best. Your boss deserves your best work ethic!

In others words "Who is your boss?" He/she is the one in charge! Listen to your boss. And...as you listen to your boss, you might find that you will have an opportunity to help your boss be the best!

And if we keep the balance...your boss will also have that opportunity to help you be more successful!

Scriptures, Thoughts and Questions:

Matthew 6:24; Luke 16:13

You either serve God...or...you serve physical things in life. You get to choose!

Deuteronomy 6

The Lord is one God. Period!

Matthew 17:5; Mark 9:7; Luke 9:35

God speaks very clearly to us when He identifies His only Son as someone that we are to pay attention to or to listen. God is very clear when He identifies His Son, Jesus. He identified Jesus at His birth. He identified Jesus at His baptism. He identified Jesus on the mount when He met with Moses and Elijah. He identified Jesus at His crucifixion, His death, His resurrection and His ascension.

John 20:27-28

Thomas was in the upper room and saw Jesus after His Resurrection. All Jesus had to do was to appear before Thomas and have him look at His hands, His feet, and His side for Thomas to realize who Jesus was. The angels tell Mary who Jesus is after His resurrection.

I Corinthians 10:31; Romans 14:7-12

We live our lives for God. No matter what we do, we will be held accountable to God.

Acts 9:3-6

Jesus even identified Himself numerous times to His followers and even to Saul, who wasn't a follower, yet.

Ephesians 6:9

Our boss's boss is in Heaven.

Chapter Nineteen Questions

1. Who is your boss?

2. Who is your boss's, Boss?

3. How do you relate to your boss?

4. When Moses writes in Deuteronomy 6 that the Lord your God is One...how do we handle that thought in reference to who is our boss?

*As long as we
are keeping the
correct culture,
the culture that God
identifies,
we will stay on track
for God's assistance in
helping us to be
successful in our
business.*

20. Keep the Culture

AT THE BEGINNING OF this book, we mentioned that God does not change. What changes is the culture. God shows us how to work and live within each culture that we might find. Sometimes our culture even goes so far as to be at odds with what God says. So if we should keep the Culture, doesn't that sound like going against God?

Well...yes and no!

As long as we are keeping the correct culture, the culture that God identifies, we will stay on track for God's assistance in helping us to be successful in our business. We have talked about the correct culture throughout this book.

Let me remind you.

It is a culture of lifting one another up to include coworkers and bosses. Discipline is an important part of our culture. Planning is important when we let our Boss lead. Listening to our coworkers has a place. Being happy in our work is very important...and there are still others.

Remembering to always do what is right has a large part in our business culture. When we do, we will be successful.

Scriptures, Thoughts and Questions:

Matthew 5-7

The Sermon on the Mount, along with the rest of the Bible gives us a good idea of what culture we are to keep here on earth.

John 18:36

Jesus's and our rest is not in this world. We will be living in a different culture but still worshipping and praising God the Father and His Son Jesus Christ. We get a glimpse of that culture with a description of a new heaven and new earth.

Chapter Twenty Questions

1. Why is it important to keep the culture in our work place?

2. What does it mean to keep the culture in our businesses?

3. What within our business culture can be at odds with what God wants?

4. What changes in the culture of the world might we be inclined to embrace within our own business culture?

If you
want to be successful,
ask your people
to tell you
what they think.

21. Don't Surround Yourself With "Yes" People

I WOULD TELL NEW staff that I was to work directly with, that I did not want someone to be a "Yes" person. I tried to fill positions with people who could think for themselves....and people who would not be afraid to tell me if they thought I was wrong.

They knew, as did I, that I was in the position to make the final decision. They knew that I was not asking my staff to make the decision, but I wanted to see different perspectives, so I could make the proper decision. They were on board because I valued their thoughts, their opinions.

To be honest, I probably already knew the answers before I even asked. But let me give you an example of one time that I asked the question, listened to a response, and changed my way of thinking because I did listen.

I was coaching baseball at a small college in the Dallas, TX area. We were practicing a particular skill which involved base running. Now to get things straight, I played baseball in High School and College. I wasn't the best player, but I was a good player, if I say so myself. Besides having played the game, I also had taken coaching classes. But that was not all...I was also a high school umpire. All of this meant that I was someone who knew how to play the game.

All that I had to do was to impart my knowledge to my baseball players.

Anyway, I was giving instruction to my college team about a particular base running skill when one of my players, caught my attention, and with a quick motion of his body, told me that maybe there was a better way to accomplish this skill. It only took a moment for me to realize that there was a better way...and I was not teaching it!

To this day, I do not remember the particular skill, except it involved base running. However, I do remember that it was worth my while to listen to my players. They helped me to be a more successful coach, and as a result, we were more successful as a team.

A business setting is not any different. Pay attention to your staff. You may have the education and experience, but your staff also has specific experience, training and of course, a different perspective. If you want to be successful, ask your people to tell you what they think. If you do, you will reap the benefits, one of which might just be a staff who is willing to work with you so that you can be more successful.

You are not obligated to do what your staff says if you ask. Keep in mind that you are still in charge and will make the final decision. But, if you take the time to ask your staff their opinions, you may find that it will help your overall business to be more successful.

Scriptures, Thoughts and Questions:

Proverbs 1:6; Mark 3:23; Mark 4:10-11

Jesus used parables to encourage questioning for growth. He knew what the answer was when He asked the question, but He was wanting his followers to think for themselves. When you think about it, that is what God has wanted all along. He wants us to follow Him willingly. He placed us in the Garden knowing that we would be susceptible to disobedience, to sin. Yet, He desired to have us follow Him because we wanted to follow Him...not just because He told us!

Matthew 16:13; Mark 8:27

Jesus asked the question of who they thought He was...and He got various responses. He knew that he could use the questioning as a teaching opportunity.

Chapter Twenty One Questions

1. Why is it important to ask your people for input? Don't you know what you are doing?

2. How do you respond when staff input is different from the approach that you had in mind?

3. Is it possible that when you ask a question about what needs to be done, that you do not get what you would consider to be a responsible reply? How would you respond to that type of response?

*If
the rules or
regulations
inhibit positive
growth,
then
they probably need to
be changed.*

22. Following Regulations

HAVE YOU EVER BEEN in a workplace that had pages of regulations? What usually happens in this situation is that the "To Do" regulations might be outnumbered by the "Don't Do" regulations maybe two to one, or more. To be fair, some of these regulations are for your health and wellbeing...your safety...and some might be for others safety, health and wellbeing. However, there might be some regulations that exist just because someone can impose a regulation.

Does an established regulation always promote improvement? I believe that sometimes regulations hold back improvements.

I would venture to say that in such a workplace, creativity is stifled, along with productivity. Fear is probably the motivating factor!

What is one to do? The one in charge may have a problem that may be very difficult to work through.

If the rules or regulations inhibit positive growth, then they probably need to be changed. Does this mean that it is OK to not follow them? I would suggest that rather than not follow a regulation, it might be best to affect change in the regulations. Just be aware of the process needed to officially make the change. Keep in mind that as the boss, you may be responsible for your staff not following regulations.

In today's workplace culture, having to follow regulations seems to be the "norm". Maybe, there are too many!

Scriptures, Thoughts and Questions:

Genesis 3

When God placed Adam and Eve in the Garden, he basically had just one regulation for the occupants. They could eat from any tree in the Garden with the exception of one tree...the Tree of the Knowledge of Good and Evil. God had only established one regulation. It seems like God might be saying that fewer regulations are better than many!

Exodus 20:1-20

When Moses went up the mountain as God commanded him, he chatted with God about His people. When he came down the mountain, he brought ten regulations with him, written by God Himself with His finger.

Daniel 1:1-21

The king had given a regulation that Daniel and his friends could not accept, so he asked for permission to make a change for a period of time. This was approved and Daniel showed improvement because he did not follow the king's rules.

Matthew 15:1-9; Matthew 12:1-13

There were many rules and regulations that the religious leaders had imposed on the people. Jesus did not agree with all of those rules. He knew how to respond to the religious leaders in a positive way.

Chapter Twenty Two Questions

1. What rules, regulations, laws, etc....do you have in your workplace that are difficult to follow? Why?

2. Do you have the option in your work to set aside a regulation?

3. Do you have any regulations in your workplace that might not promote improvement or success?

4. Do you have a process to follow if a rule or regulation needs to be changed?

*The key
to making your boss
look good along
with your coworkers
is to do what is
right...
in your work...
with your
coworkers... and with
your boss!*

23. Make Your Staff (and Your Boss) Look Good

IF YOU GET AN opportunity, take a good long look at a successful business, or even several. Think about what makes that business a success!

Look at the workers. What attitude do they have? How are they treated by their bosses? Do they appear to want to work in that work place?

What about their work place? Is it a place that encourages people to work? Are the workers friendly toward one another? Do the workers smile while they work? Do the workers seem to know their jobs? Are the workers focused on moving in the right direction, or are they confused?

What about the bosses? How do they treat their staff? Do the bosses encourage new ideas, without throwing out the old? Have the bosses expressed the vision of the work place in a clear fashion? Do the bosses appear to enjoy their work? Do the bosses treat their staff fairly? What direction do the bosses try to move the entire business?

The key to making your boss look good along with your coworkers is to do what is right... in your work... with your coworkers... and with your boss!

When you do this...you will have taken the opportunity to make success happen.

Scriptures, Thoughts and Questions:

We who are strong in faith should help the weak with their weaknesses, and not please only ourselves. 2 Let each of us please our neighbors for their good, to help them be stronger in faith. **(Romans 15:1-2, NCV)**

2 Chronicles 7:3

The people worshipped and thanked the Lord saying the Lord is good.

Job 2:3

Job makes God look good by his actions. As a result, God speaks highly of Job.

Isaiah 63:7 ff

The people make God look good when they praise Him and ask Him to do for them what they cannot do themselves. They put their faith in Him and depend upon Him.

Chapter Twenty Three Questions

1. How can you make your boss look good?

2. How can you make your boss look bad?

3. What kind of attitude do you need to have to make someone else look good in your work?

4. Is it important to thank the boss in front of other co-workers?

5. What does it mean to put your faith in your boss?

6. Can you make your boss look good when you take the opportunity to make a co-worker look good?

7. What happens to your boss when you make the boss look good?

...establishing good relationships is exactly what someone needs to be successful in business (and in Life).

Epilogue

THERE ARE MANY SCRIPTURES that relate to being successful. These concepts apply to business or whatever you do. The concepts about being successful are there, even if the main idea in the verse may be talking about something else. That is the marvelous wonder of God's Word...you can come away with more than one positive thought, even from the same passage.

It seems like most of the advice that is found in scriptures has to do with establishing good relationships...relationships with your family, your friends, your work and most importantly, with Jesus Christ. In essence, establishing good relationships is exactly what someone needs to be successful in business.

I have provided a few more varied scriptures that might be helpful. Think on them because they will help you to be successful, not only in business, but in life. You can find management concepts throughout scripture and the following are only a few.

I Samuel 18:14

David had great success in everything he did because the Lord was with him.

This verse is about David. He had already been anointed King, but he was currently in the service of King Saul who hated David because the Lord was with him. This verse speaks to success in our own lives.

II Chronicles 26:1-23

This chapter is about Uzziah, King of Judah who as long as he did what was right and what God asked of him, God blessed him and Uzziah had success. When he got older, he forgot that God had blessed him and he let his pride take over. We need to remember the people in our business that help to make us successful. If we become prideful of what we do, then we will begin to fail.

Ruth 1-4

These four chapters describe the process for success. Everything is done in the proper order and according to the rules. When completed, Ruth had a new husband and Boaz had a new wife. Ruth paid attention to Naomi and Ruth learned from her. The end result was success which led to the birth of David, the future King of Israel.

Acts 1:21-25

These verses show a process of promoting one of their own. The Apostles laid down the rules to establish the process and they selected one who was not a novice, but one who definitely had experience.

Exodus 18:13-27

Moses, as the leader, listened to the people's problems and complaints. This took a large amount of his time so his father in Law, Jethro, gave him some advice. This advice was to appoint leaders of the people who would be in charge of groups so that Moses would only hear the major complaints, problems, etc....and his appointed leaders would listen to and provide solutions to the smaller groups. This would free Moses up so he could spend more time in communication with God about the people. Moses had to be willing to listen when a problem was evident to others. The advice given was that Moses was working too hard and would wear himself out, if he did not make changes. It is important to sometimes take a step back and look at the big picture. By making the suggested changes, Moses elevated other good people into leadership positions and actually prepared them for the future. This was success.

Acts 15

Some new Jewish Christians felt like the gentiles needed to become Jews or at least to follow Jewish rules to become Christians. These individuals followed Paul on his first missionary journey and posed problems. So Paul and his companions went to Jerusalem to ask advice from the leaders of the Church. The Apostles listened to both sides of the issue, discussed various aspects of what God was doing, and made a decision which they put in writing. This letter was then sent to all the new churches so old and new alike understood what God, the big Boss, wanted.

www.ingramcontent.com/pod-product-compliance
Lightning Source LLC
Chambersburg PA
CBHW060832050426
42453CB00008B/663